NBA CHAMPIONSHIPS:

↓

1989, 1990, 2004

↓

ALL-TIME LEADING SCORER:

↓

ISIAH THOMAS (1981–94):

↓

18,822 POINTS

ETROIT
5
HEAT
0

THE NBA: A HISTORY OF HOOPS

DETROIT PISTONS

BY JIM WHITING

CREATIVE EDUCATION CREATIVE PAPERBACKS

Published by Creative Education
and Creative Paperbacks

P.O. Box 227, Mankato, Minnesota 56002

Creative Education and Creative Paperbacks
are imprints of The Creative Company

www.thecreativecompany.us

Design and production by Blue Design

Printed in the United States of America

Photographs by AP Images (ASSOCIATED PRESS), Corbis (Bettmann), Getty Images (Glen Allison, Andrew D. Bernstein/NBAE, Richard Cummins, Scott Cunningham/NBAE, Allen Einstein/NBAE, Focus on Sport, Rob Foldy/Getty Images Sport, George Gojkovich, Andy Hayt/NBAE, Harry How/Getty Images Sport, David E. Klutho/Sports Illustrated, George Long/Sports Illustrated, Manny Millan/Sports Illustrated, Jason Miller/Getty Images Sport, NBA Photos/NBAE, Dick Raphael/NBAE, Jerry Wachter/Sports Illustrated), Newscom (CURTIS COMPTON/MCT, Chris Szagola/Cal Sport Media)

Library of Congress Cataloging-in-Publication Data

Names: Whiting, Jim, 1943- author.

Title: Detroit Pistons / Jim Whiting.

Series: The NBA: A History of Hoops.

Includes bibliographical references and index.

Summary: This high-interest title summarizes the history of the Detroit Pistons professional basketball team, highlighting memorable events and noteworthy players such as Isiah Thomas.

Identifiers: LCCN 2016054008 / ISBN 978-1-60818-843-7 (hardcover) / ISBN 978-1-62832-446-4 (pbk) / ISBN 978-1-56660-891-6 (eBook)

Subjects: LCSH: 1. Detroit Pistons (Basketball team)—History—Juvenile literature.
2. Detroit Pistons (Basketball team)—Biography—Juvenile literature.

Classification: LCC GV885.52.D47 W45 2017 / DDC 796.323/640977434—dc23

CCSS: RI.4.1, 2, 3, 4; RI.5.1, 2, 4; RI.6.1, 2, 3; RF.4.3, 4; RF.5.3, 4; RH. 6-8. 4, 5, 7

First Edition HC 9 8 7 6 5 4 3 2 1

First Edition PBK 9 8 7 6 5 4 3 2 1

State F
adidas
DETROIT
adidas

LAKERS
PISTONS
10
PISTONS
40

CONTENTS

Home to the Ford Motor Company since 1903, **DETROIT** is known as "Motor City."

BLUE-COLLAR BASKETBALL

Game 2 of the 2004 National Basketball Association (NBA) Eastern Conference finals series between the Detroit Pistons and Indiana Pacers was intense and low-scoring. The teams combined for

TAYSHAUN PRINCE famously sacrificed his body to block a Pacers win in 2004.

26 blocked shots. The final one might be the greatest blocked shot in NBA playoff history. Detroit clung to a 69–67 lead. Twenty seconds remained. Indiana stole the ball. Guard Reggie Miller streaked toward the basket. No Piston was within 15 feet of him. Miller jumped for what seemed to be an easy layup. It would tie the score. Indiana would have a chance to win in overtime. It already had a one-game lead in the series. Winning again would give the Pacers a huge advantage. From out of nowhere, Pistons forward Tayshaun Prince slashed toward Miller. He swatted the ball away. Prince's momentum carried him several rows into the crowd. "There is no way he should be able to get to this shot," said the TV announcer. "No way. He just laid it out." Detroit won, 72–67. The Pistons went on to take the series. Then they dominated the Los Angeles Lakers in five games to win the NBA championship. Prince's hustle and willingness to sacrifice his body showed the grit and determination that characterize the Pistons. No wonder Detroit is known as the home of "blue-collar basketball."

INDIANA
31
DETROIT
22
DETROIT
32
CONSECO
THE FINAL

Point guard **GENE SHUE** was a five-time All-Star with the Pistons from 1957 to 1962.

LEGENDS OF THE HARDWOOD

WE'LL PLAY ANYWHERE

In the early days of the NBL, teams played in high school gyms, armories, and ballrooms. "In those days, you would drive into town and look for the biggest building," said Buddy Jeannette, one of the team's stars. Once, he rushed into a bar in a town where the Pistons were supposed to play. He asked the bartender where the game was. "Right here," the man replied. "After we got dressed they had shoved all the tables back and put a basket on one wall, and on the other side they had a basket drawn up into the ceiling," Jeannette said.

ONE PLAYER SAID, "I NEVER REALLY SAW THE FANS GET PHYSICAL WITH THE PLAYERS. I HAD THEM PULL THE HAIR ON MY LEGS, THOUGH."

For the Pistons, "blue collar" is true. The team's original owner was Fred Zollner. He owned a piston manufacturing company in Fort Wayne, Indiana. Pistons are the parts that move up and down in engine blocks in cars and trucks. They generate the power that propels these vehicles. In 1939, Zollner formed the Fort Wayne Zollner Pistons. Two years later the Zollner Pistons joined the National Basketball League (NBL). Most arenas in the league were small. Some held just a few hundred people. Spectators might be within a foot or two of the court. One player said, "I never really saw the fans get physical with the players. I had them pull the hair on my legs, though." The Pistons were league champs in 1944 and 1945. Bobby McDermott was the team's leading scorer. Al Cervi, who often guarded him, said, "Oh, he

FT. WAYNE 12
FT. WAYNE 15
ZOLLNER 7 PISTONS
ZOLLNER 18 PISTONS
FT. WAYNE 17
FT. WAYNE 16
FT. WAYNE 18
ZOLLNER 8 PISTONS
FT. WAYNE 7
ZOLLNER 10 PISTONS
ZOLLNER 6 PISTONS
ZOLLNER 15 PISTONS
FT. WAYNE 14
FT. WAYNE 8

The Fort Wayne **ZOLLNER PISTONS** topped the NBL for two years during the 1940s.

could shoot! If he shot 10 times from 30 feet, I'd guarantee he'd make 8 in game conditions." *Collier's* magazine made him part of an "All-World" team in 1950.

In 1948, officials of the rival Basketball Association of America (BAA) approached Zollner. They invited him to join their league. BAA teams played in much larger arenas. Zollner liked the idea of giving his team more exposure. He also thought the BAA was more businesslike in its operations. The Pistons struggled in the new league. They had a 22–38 record. The following year, the two leagues merged to form the NBA. In an era before TV contracts, some teams struggled financially. Zollner provided his own money to keep the league afloat. He also shared ideas that helped popularize the league.

MOVING TO MOTOWN

The Pistons did well in their first NBA season. They finished 40–28. They won the first round of the playoffs. Then the Minneapolis Lakers defeated them in the division finals. In that season, the NBA

Forward **GEORGE YARDLEY** set a team single-game scoring record with 52 points.

had 17 teams. It was down to 11 by the start of the 1950–51 season. The Pistons had losing records in that season and the following one. In 1954, Zollner became the first—and still only—NBA owner to hire a former referee as head coach. Charley Eckman's only officiating experience was with Army Air Force teams during World War II. "It sounded crazy at first, but then I figured I had nothing to lose," Eckman said. "I had $38 to my name after spending all winter running around the country officiating high school, college, and pro games. I also had a wife and three kids with big appetites. Why not take a shot at it?"

Eckman had a talented team led by star forward George "Bird" Yardley and center Larry Foust. In Eckman's first season, the Pistons won the Western Division with a 43–29 record. They advanced to the NBA Finals against the Syracuse Nationals. They blew

LEGENDS OF THE HARDWOOD

THE FRIENDLY SKIES

In 1952, Fred Zollner bought an airplane. He named it the "Flying Z." It was the first time an owner purchased a plane to carry an entire team. Flying allowed the Pistons to arrive in plenty of time to get a good night's sleep before games. They didn't have to endure long, uncomfortable train trips. The other teams envied the Pistons. The "Flying Z" had comfortable furniture, a galley, and tables where coaches and players could play cards. Zollner personally hated making air trips, though. "He was a real 'white-knuckler' when it came to flying," said general manager Carl Bennett.

LARRY FOUST and the Pistons came up against the Warriors in the 1956 Finals.

a 17-point lead in Game 7 and lost by 1 point. The Pistons returned to the Finals the following year. The Philadelphia Warriors beat them four games to one.

By this time, NBA teams in midsized cities were having financial problems. Their populations seemed too small to compete with the big-city teams. Fort Wayne was no exception. It was the league's smallest city. During the 1956–57 season, Zollner Company treasurer Otto Adams said, "We are no different from several other NBA cities—Minneapolis, Rochester, and Syracuse—which are looking around for future sites because present attendance suggests such action." With rumors swirling about a possible move, fans stayed away. The unease spread to the court. The team limped into the playoffs. They lost in the first round. By then, Zollner had announced that the team would move

Pistons owner Fred Zollner moved the team to Detroit before the 1957–58 season.

to Detroit. The "Motor City" was the automotive capital of the country. The team kept the Pistons nickname. The Zollner part was dropped. "I feel a club can do better in a metropolitan area of 2 million people than an area of 200,000," Zollner said. "Detroit has long been one of America's great sports centers, and the Detroit Pistons will round out a program of having a pennant contender in professional basketball to go along with the Detroit Tigers, Detroit Lions, and Detroit Red Wings."

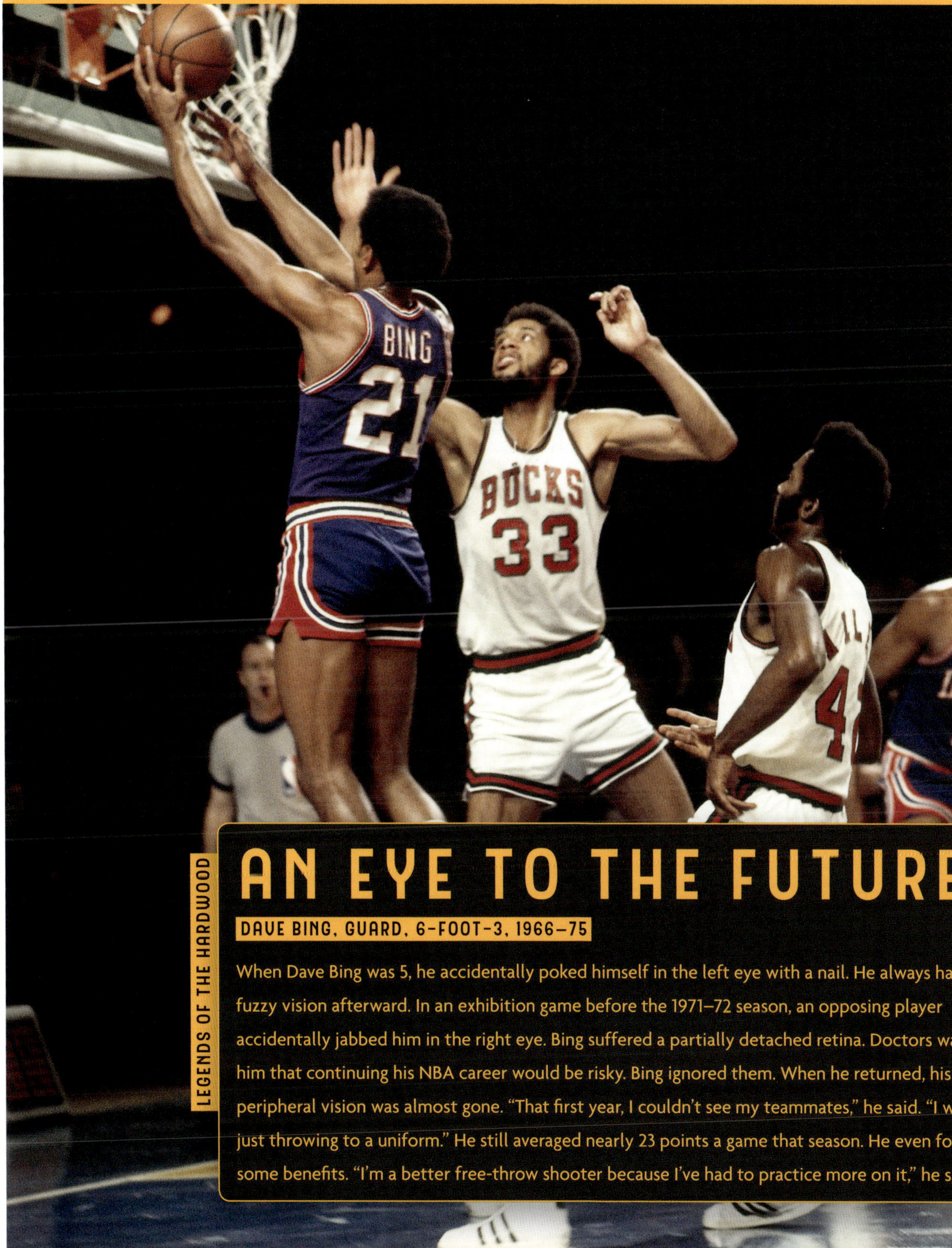

LEGENDS OF THE HARDWOOD

AN EYE TO THE FUTURE

DAVE BING, GUARD, 6-FOOT-3, 1966–75

When Dave Bing was 5, he accidentally poked himself in the left eye with a nail. He always had fuzzy vision afterward. In an exhibition game before the 1971–72 season, an opposing player accidentally jabbed him in the right eye. Bing suffered a partially detached retina. Doctors warned him that continuing his NBA career would be risky. Bing ignored them. When he returned, his peripheral vision was almost gone. "That first year, I couldn't see my teammates," he said. "I was just throwing to a uniform." He still averaged nearly 23 points a game that season. He even found some benefits. "I'm a better free-throw shooter because I've had to practice more on it," he said.

DOWN DAYS IN DETROIT

Detroit had been home to several other professional hoops teams. None lasted long. The Detroit Eagles played in the NBL from 1939 to 1941. The Detroit Gems joined the NBL in 1946. They went just

A Detroit native, forward **DAVE DeBUSSCHERE** played tough defense and reliable offense.

Intimidating center **BOB LANIER** possessed a deadly combination of skill and strength.

"YOU CAN'T OPEN UP A MAN'S CHEST AND LOOK AT HIS HEART, BUT I GUARANTEE THERE'S ONE BIG [HEART] BEATING IN BING," SAID BOSTON CELTICS COACH RED AUERBACH.

4–40 and moved to Minneapolis. The Detroit Falcons joined the BAA the same year. They folded in 1947. The Detroit Vagabond Kings joined the NBL in 1948. They won just 2 of their 19 games. They also disbanded.

The Pistons continued this "tradition" of losing basketball in the Motor City. They went 33–39 in 1957–58. The NBA was now down to only eight teams. Six made the playoffs. The Pistons won the first round but lost to the St. Louis Hawks in the division finals. Yardley provided a rare bright spot. His 2,001 points led the league. It was the first time a player had reached the 2,000-point milestone. The cycle continued for five seasons. The Pistons posted losing records. They almost always suffered first-round defeat.

The situation grew even worse in 1963–64. The league had added a ninth team two years earlier. Detroit finished with the worst record in the Western Division. It missed the playoffs. The Pistons tried another coaching experiment the following season. Power forward Dave DeBusschere became player/coach. At just 24, he was the youngest coach in NBA history. Unlike Eckman, he couldn't get his team into the playoffs. He turned over his coaching duties to an assistant during the 1966–67 season. The next year, he teamed with guard Dave Bing to help the Pistons go 40–42. Detroit returned to the playoffs. Bing had joined the team in 1966. He averaged 20 points a game then and was named Rookie of the Year. "You can't open up a man's chest and look at his

Guard **ERIC MONEY** averaged nearly 12 points a game over 5 seasons in Detroit.

heart, but I guarantee there's one big [heart] beating in Bing," said Boston Celtics coach Red Auerbach. "Give me one man like Dave Bing, and I'll build a championship team around him."

Detroit couldn't do that. The Pistons kept putting on the brakes. They finally had a winning season in 1970–71. But the team's 45–37 mark wasn't good enough for the playoffs. It went back to losing records in the next two years. Massive center Bob Lanier helped Detroit to a winning record in 1973–74. At the end of the season, Zollner sold the team to Detroit businessman William Davidson. Another winning mark in 1976–77 gave hope to the team's long-suffering fans. But the Pistons returned to their losing ways for the next six seasons. The low point came during 1979–80. Detroit won just 16 games. But brighter days lay ahead.

LEGENDS OF THE HARDWOOD

IT'S RAINING BASKETS

DETROIT PISTONS AT DENVER NUGGETS, DECEMBER 13, 1983

"If you go to Denver, you know you're going to be in for a scoring match," said Detroit's Kelly Tripucka. "They didn't run a lot of plays, they just kept running." The score was 145–145 at the end of regulation time. The first overtime ended in a tie. So did the second. "The game lasted so long, we were wondering if we could find a place to eat after the game," Tripucka said. "We were wondering, 'is there an all-night diner in Denver?'" Detroit finally pulled ahead in the third overtime. They won 186–184. It is the highest-scoring game in NBA history.

A physical center who brawled beneath the basket, **BILL LAIMBEER** led Detroit in rebounds.

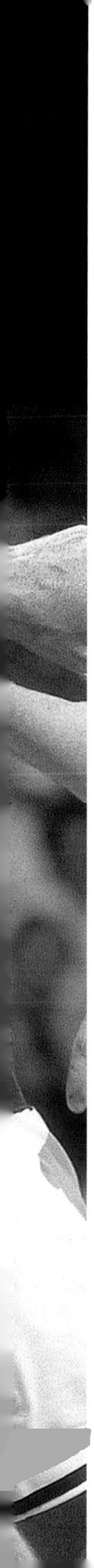

BIRTH OF THE BAD BOYS

The Pistons began laying the foundation for success in the 1981 NBA Draft. Detroit selected point guard Isiah Thomas with the second overall pick. "I believe God made people to perform

ISIAH THOMAS retired as the franchise's all-time leader in points, assists, and steals.

certain acts," said Pistons official Will Robinson. "Frank Sinatra was made to sing, Jesse Owens was made to run, and Isiah Thomas was made to play basketball." They also drafted high-scoring forward Kelly Tripucka. The team traded for muscular guard Vinnie Johnson and tough center Bill Laimbeer during the 1981–82 season. When Detroit hired coach Chuck Daly to start the 1983–84 season, it was "pedal to the metal." Detroit enjoyed three straight winning seasons, though each one ended with early playoff exits. But the Pistons souped up their engine with key additions. They drafted little-known guard Joe Dumars in 1985. Then they drafted center John Salley and rebounding specialist Dennis Rodman. They traded for hefty power forward/center Rick Mahorn. Coach Daly taught an aggressive style of defense. The Pistons played tough. They played hard. Many people thought they played dirty. The media called them the "Bad Boys." They often wore black jerseys with an image of a skull and crossbones when they practiced.

The Pistons won 52 games in 1986–87. They raced through their first two playoff rounds. They narrowly lost to Boston in the conference finals, four games to three. The next year, they advanced to the NBA Finals against the Lakers. They won three of the first five games. Thomas scored a Finals-record 25 points in the third quarter of Game 6. It wasn't quite enough. The Lakers won that game 103–102. Then they won Game 7.

PISTONS
BULLS
14

LEGENDS OF THE HARDWOOD

MAN OF MANY NAMES

VINNIE JOHNSON, POINT GUARD/SHOOTING GUARD, 6-FOOT-2, 1981–91

Vinnie Johnson had several nicknames. The most famous is "Microwave." He would "heat up" as soon as he came off the bench and score often. Teammates called him "The Who." In practice, he often shouted, "Heee! Wooo!" when he scored. He earned "007" when he sank a jump shot with 00.7 second remaining in Game 5 of the 1990 Finals against the Portland Trail Blazers. Afterward, he liked to pose for pictures in which he resembled James Bond, the original 007. Yet another nickname was "Brooklyn Bridge." Johnson grew up in Brooklyn and often leaned forward like a bridge when shooting jumpers.

The Pistons picked up another "Bad Boy" during the 1988–89 season. Mark Aguirre had starred for the Dallas Mavericks. He played as if he were always angry. He argued with teammates and coaches. That made him a perfect fit in Detroit. Detroit posted the NBA's best record that season, 63–19. It lost only two games in the first three playoff rounds. The team capped the season by sweeping the Lakers in four games. It was Detroit's first NBA championship. Dumars was named the Most Valuable Player (MVP) of the Finals. "Dumars wouldn't miss," said Mitch Kupchak, a Lakers team official. "It was as if he had forgotten how."

The Pistons were nearly as good the following year. They won 59 games. They sped to the Finals to face the Portland Trail Blazers. They won their second straight title! Isiah Thomas earned Finals MVP honors. He passed along the credit. "There is no way we would have won two championships in Detroit if Mark Aguirre's not on that team," he said years later.

The Pistons had beaten Michael Jordan and the Chicago Bulls in the playoffs for three straight years. The Bulls turned the tables in 1990–91. They beat Detroit in the conference finals. Detroit suffered through three losing seasons from 1992–93 to 1994–95. Most of the Bad Boys moved on. Their era was over.

A THIRD TITLE

Detroit's rise to NBA power wasn't over. The Pistons made the playoffs in four of the next six seasons, but they didn't get beyond the first round. Once again, though, they were retooling the engine of a championship team. Center Ben Wallace arrived in a trade in 2000. He would go on to earn four Defensive

"BIG BEN" WALLACE led the league in total rebounds in 2000–01 and 2002–03.

Guard **RICHARD "RIP" HAMILTON** led Detroit to the playoffs in seven seasons.

"WE DIDN'T WORRY ABOUT WHAT PEOPLE WROTE IN THE PAPERS OR WHAT PEOPLE WERE SAYING ON TV," SAID HAMILTON. "WE SAID TO OURSELVES, 'ANYTHING IS POSSIBLE IF YOU PLAY TOGETHER AS FIVE.'"

Player of the Year awards. Two years later, the Pistons drafted Tayshaun Prince. They also traded for point guard Chauncey Billups and small forward/shooting guard Richard "Rip" Hamilton.

They added power forward/center Rasheed Wallace late in the 2003–04 season. He was the last piece of the puzzle. The Pistons powered to the Finals. They faced the heavily favored Lakers for the championship. "We didn't worry about what people wrote in the papers or what people were saying on TV," said Hamilton. "We said to ourselves, 'Anything is possible if you play together as five.'" They toppled the Lakers in five games for their third NBA title.

CENTERPIECE

LEGENDS OF THE HARDWOOD

ANDRE DRUMMOND, CENTER, 7 FEET, 2012–PRESENT

In middle school, Andre Drummond was tall. He *looked* like a basketball player. He didn't *play* like one. "I was all over the place, tripping over myself, falling on the court," he said. His seventh-grade coach cut him. Drummond went to his local YMCA. "I played pickup there from dawn to dusk," he explained. Slowly he improved. The Pistons selected him as the ninth overall selection in the 2012 NBA Draft. When Stan Van Gundy took over, he built the team around Drummond. In 3 of the first 6 games of 2015–16, Drummond tallied 20 points and 20 rebounds. The only other players to accomplish that feat were Kareem Abdul-Jabbar and Wilt Chamberlain.

High-energy point guard **BRANDON JENNINGS** provided solid scoring and rebounding.

The Pistons nearly repeated as champions the following season. They returned to the Finals. But the San Antonio Spurs defeated Detroit, four games to three. The Pistons raced to a franchise-best 64 wins in 2005–06. But the Miami Heat set up a roadblock in the conference finals. The following two seasons followed the same pattern, with losses in the conference finals. Trading Billups during the 2008–09 season disrupted the team chemistry. The Pistons plunged to 39–43. They still qualified for the playoffs. But they were eliminated in the first round. That loss started another downward spiral. In the next 6 seasons,

Guard **RODNEY STUCKEY** helped propel the Pistons to 59 wins and the playoffs in 2008.

the Pistons ranged from a high of 32 wins to a low of 25.

Before the 2014–15 season, Detroit hired Stan Van Gundy as coach. He had taken both Miami and Orlando to the playoffs. “We will work to put a team on the floor that reflects the franchise’s rich tradition and embodies the toughness and work ethic of fans in the Detroit area,” he said. Detroit added point guard Reggie Jackson late in the season. He averaged nearly 18 points a game. Jackson became the first Pistons player in nearly 20 years to have multiple triple-doubles. (A triple-

Forward **MARCUS MORRIS** boosted Detroit in 2015–16 with 14 points per game.

After joining the Pistons, **REGGIE JACKSON** worked hard to improve his shot.

"OUR ATTITUDE IS FORGED FROM ADVERSITY AND A BOND THAT OTHERS WOULDN'T UNDERSTAND."

double is when a player gets double-digit tallies in three categories.) One of Jackson's favorite passing targets was center Andre Drummond. He averaged nearly 14 points and 13 rebounds a game in 2013–14 and 2014–15. Drummond put up even bigger numbers in 2015–16. The Pistons finished the season with 44 wins. They finally returned to the playoffs. But they fell to Cleveland in the first round. A repeat performance proved elusive, however, as the Pistons fell to 37–45 the next season. Detroit missed the playoffs for the seventh time in eight years.

Like pistons in a car engine, basketball in Detroit has gone up. Then down. Up. Down. Up. It has gone down for several years. But the Pistons remained confident as they prepared to move into Little Caesars Arena in 2017–18. With one of the NBA's younger rosters, Detroit looks to start another upward cycle. Fans hope it will drive them to another championship.

SELECTED BIBLIOGRAPHY

Ballard, Chris. *The Art of a Beautiful Game: The Thinking Fan's Tour of the NBA*. New York: Simon & Schuster, 2010.

Hubbard, Jan, ed. *The Official NBA Basketball Encyclopedia*. 3rd edition. New York: Doubleday, 2000.

NBA.com. "Detroit Pistons." http://www.nba.com/pistons.

Nelson, Rodger. *The Zollner Piston Story*. 1995. https://archive.org/stream/zollnerpistonsto00nels/zollnerpistonsto00nels_djvu.txt.

Simmons, Bill. *The Book of Basketball: The NBA According to the Sports Guy*. New York: Ballantine, 2009.

WEBSITES

DUCKSTERS BASKETBALL: NBA

http://www.ducksters.com/sports/national_basketball_association.php

Learn more about NBA history, rules, positions, strategy, drills, and other topics.

TAYSHAUN PRINCE—THE GREATEST BLOCK IN NBA PLAYOFF HISTORY

https://www.youtube.com/watch?v=8QJ4iwqnLKc

Watch a three-minute video of Tayshaun Prince's spectacular blocked shot.

Note: Every effort has been made to ensure that any websites listed above were active at the time of publication. However, because of the nature of the Internet, it is impossible to guarantee that these sites will remain active indefinitely or that their contents will not be altered.

INDEX